MW00639775

How to Make Money in Stocks:

RULES FOR INVESTMENT SUCCESS

BY SIR JOHN TEMPLETON

These principles appeared in 1993 in World Monitor: The Christian Science Monitor Monthly. While market and economic data included in this 1993 article are obviously outdated, Sir John Templeton's core investment principles are still relevant.

CONTENTS

Sir John Templeton

Sir John Templeton was an investor and mutual fund pioneer. He was born in the town of Winchester, Tennessee, and attended Yale University, where he was an assistant business manager for campus humor magazine Yale Record and was selected for membership in the Elihu society. He financed a portion of his tuition by playing poker, a game at which he excelled.

He graduated in 1934 near the top of his class. He attended Oxford University as a Rhodes scholar and earned an M.A. in law.

Templeton married Judith Folk in 1937, and the couple had three children: John Jr., Anne, and Christopher. Judith died in February 1951 in a motorbike accident. He remarried, to Irene Reynolds Butler in 1958; she died in 1993.

He was a lifelong member of the Presbyterian Church. He served as an elder of the First Presbyterian Church of Englewood (NJ). He was a trustee on the board of Princeton Theological Seminary, the largest Presbyterian seminary, for 42 years and served as its chair for 12 years.

Templeton became a billionaire by pioneering the use of globally diversified mutual funds. His Templeton Growth Fund, Ltd. (investment fund), established in 1954, was among the first who invested in Japan in the middle of the 1960s.

He is noted for, during the Depression of the 1930s, buying 100 shares of each NYSE listed company, which was then selling for less than $1 a share ($17 today) (104 companies, in 1939), later making many times the money back when the USA industry picked up as a result of World War II.

In 2006, he was listed in a seven-way tie for 129th place on the Sunday Times' "Rich List". He rejected technical analysis for stock trading, preferring instead to use fundamental analysis. Money magazine in 1999 called him "arguably the greatest global stock picker of the century".

Templeton was one of the most generous philanthropists in history, giving away over

$1 billion to charitable causes. Templeton renounced his US citizenship in 1964, thus allowing him to channel an additional $100 million that he would have paid in US income taxes when he sold his international investment fund, toward philanthropy. He had dual naturalized Bahamian and British citizenship and lived in the Bahamas.

As a philanthropist, Templeton established:

The John Templeton Foundation;

The Templeton Prize for Progress Toward Research or Discoveries about Spiritual Realities in 1972;

The Templeton Library in Sewanee, Tennessee; and

The Templeton College of the University of Oxford (by endowing the Oxford Centre for Management Studies to become a full college of the university having as a focus business and management studies).

Templeton College is now closely associated with Oxford's Saïd Business School. In 2007, Templeton College transferred its executive education program to Saïd Business School. In 2008, Templeton College merged with Green College to form Green Templeton College.[17] This is one of the exceptional mergers in recent history of the University of Oxford.

He was created a Knight Bachelor in 1987 for his philanthropic efforts. Templeton was inducted into the Junior Achievement US Business Hall of Fame in 1996, and in 2003 awarded the William E. Simon Prize.

His philanthropic activities had been estimated at over 1 billion US dollars in total.

In 2007, Templeton was named one of Time magazine's 100 Most Influential People (Time 100) under the category of "Power Givers." Templeton was given this honor for his "pursuit of spiritual understanding, often through scientific research" through his establishment of the John Templeton Foundation.

Templeton attributed much of his success to his ability to maintain an elevated mood, avoid anxiety, and stay disciplined. Uninterested in consumerism, he drove his own car, never flew first class, and lived year-round in the Bahamas.

Templeton became known for his "avoiding the herd" and "buy when there's blood in the streets" philosophy. He was also known for taking profits when values and expectations were high.

Templeton was a Chartered Financial Analyst (CFA) charter-holder. He received AIMR's first award for professional excellence in 1991.

In 2005, he wrote a brief memorandum predicting that within five years there would be financial chaos in the world. It was eventually made public in 2010.

On 8 July 2008, Templeton died at Doctors Hospital in Nassau, Bahamas, of pneumonia at 12:20 local time. He was 95.

RULES FOR INVESTMENT SUCCESS

I can sum up my message by reminding you of Will Rogers' famous advice.

"Don't gamble," he said. "Buy some good stock. Hold it till it goes up...and then sell it.

If it doesn't go up, don't buy it!"

There is as much wisdom as humor in this remark. Success in the stock market is based on the principle of buying low and selling high. Granted, one can make money by reversing the order, selling high and then buying low. And there is money to be made in those strange animals, options, and futures. But these are techniques for traders and speculators, not for investors. And I am writing as a professional investor, one who has enjoyed a certain degree of success as an investment counselor over the past half-century and who wishes to share with others the lessons learned during this time.

N° 1

INVEST FOR MAXIMUM
TOTAL REAL RETURN

This means the return on invested dollars after taxes and after inflation. This is the only rational objective for most long-term investors. Any investment strategy that fails to recognize the insidious effect of taxes and inflation fails to recognize the true nature of the investment environment; thus, is severely handicapped.

It is vital that you protect purchasing power. One of the biggest mistakes people make is putting too much money into fixed-income securities.

Today's dollar buys only what 35 cents bought in the mid 1970s, what 21 cents bought in 1960, and what 15 cents bought after World War II. U.S. consumer prices have risen every one of the last 38 years.

If inflation averages 4%, it will reduce the buying power of a $100,000 portfolio to $68,000 in just 10 years. In other words, to

maintain the same buying power, that portfolio would have to grow to $147,000, a 47%
gain simply to remain even over a decade.
And this doesn't even count taxes.

"Diversify. In stocks and bonds, as in much
else, there is safety in numbers.

N° 2

INVEST; DON'T TRADE
OR SPECULATE

The stock market is not a casino, but if you move in and out of stocks every time they move a point or two, or if you continually sell short... or deal only in options...or trade in futures...the market will be your casino. And, like most gamblers, you may lose eventually or frequently.

You may find your profits consumed by commissions. You may find a market you expected to turn down turning up and up, and up in defiance of all your careful calculations and short sales. Every time a Wall Street news announcer says, "This just in," your heart will stop.

Keep in mind the wise words of Lucien Hooper, a Wall Street legend: "What always impresses me," he wrote, "is how much better the relaxed, long-term owners of stock do with their portfolios than the traders do with their switching of inventory. The relaxed investor is usually better informed and more understanding of essential values; he is more patient and less emotional; he pays smaller capital gains taxes; he does not incur unnecessary brokerage commissions; and he avoids behaving like Cassius by 'thinking too much.'"

N° 3

REMAIN FLEXIBLE AND OPEN-MINDED ABOUT TYPES OF INVESTMENT

There are times to buy blue chip stocks, cyclical stocks, corporate bonds, U.S. Treasury instruments, and so on. And there are times to sit on cash, because sometimes cash enables you to take advantage of investment opportunities.

The fact is there is no one kind of investment that is always best. If a particular industry or type of security becomes popular with investors, that popularity will always prove temporary and when lost, may not return for many years.

Having said that, I should note that, for most of the time, most of our clients' money has been in common stocks. A look at history will show why. From January of 1946 through June of 1991, the Dow Jones Industrial Average rose by 11.4% average annually including reinvestment of dividends, but not counting taxes compared with an average annual inflation rate of 4.4%. Had the Dow merely kept pace with inflation, it would be around 1,400 right now instead of over 3,000, a figure that seemed extreme to some 10 years ago, when I calculated that it was a very realistic possibility on the horizon.

Look also at the Standard and Poor's (S&P) Index of 500 stocks. From the start of the 1950s through the end of the 1980s four decades altogether the S&P 500 rose at an average rate of 12.5%, compared with 4.3% for inflation, 4.8% for U.S. Treasury bonds, 5.2% for Treasury bills, and 5.4% for high-grade corporate bonds.

In fact, the S&P 500 outperformed inflation, Treasury bills, and corporate bonds in every decade except the '70s, and it outperformed Treasury bonds supposedly the safest of all investments in all four decades. I repeat: There is no real safety without preserving purchasing power.

N° 4

BUY LOW

Of course, you say, that's obvious. Well, it may be, but that isn't the way the market works. When prices are high, a lot of investors are buying a lot of stocks. Prices are low when demand is low. Investors have pulled back, people are discouraged and pessimistic.

When almost everyone is pessimistic at the same time, the entire market collapses. More often, just stocks in particular fields fall. Industries such as auto making and casualty insurance go through regular cycles. Sometimes stocks of companies like the thrift institutions or money-center banks fall out of favor all at once.

Whatever the reason, investors are on the sidelines, sitting on their wallets. Yes, they tell you: "Buy low, sell high." But all too many of them bought high and sold low. Then you ask: "When will you buy the stock?" The usual answer: "Why, after analysts agree on a favorable outlook."

This is foolish, but it is human nature. It is extremely difficult to go against the crowd to buy when everyone else is selling or has sold, to buy when things look darkest, to buy when so many experts are telling you that stocks in general, or in this particular industry, or even in this particular company, are risky right now.

But, if you buy the same securities everyone else is buying, you will have the same results as everyone else. By definition, you can't outperform the market if you buy the market. And chances are if you buy what everyone is buying you will do so only after it is already overpriced.

Heed the words of the great pioneer of stock analysis, Benjamin Graham: "Buy when most people, including experts are pessimistic, and sell when they are actively optimistic."

Bernard Baruch, advisor to presidents, was even more succinct: "Never follow the crowd."

So simple in concept. So difficult in execution.

N° 5

WHEN BUYING STOCKS, SEARCH FOR BARGAINS AMONG QUALITY STOCKS

Quality is a company strongly entrenched as the sales leader in a growing market. Quality is a company that's the technological leader in a field that depends on technical innovation. Quality is a strong management team with a proven track record. Quality is a well-capitalized company that is among the first in a new market. Quality is a well-known trusted brand for a high-profit-margin consumer product.

Naturally, you cannot consider these attributes of quality in isolation. A company may be the low-cost producer, for example, but it is not a quality stock if its product line is falling out of favor with customers. Likewise, being the technological leader in a technological field means little without adequate capitalization for expansion and marketing.

Determining quality in a stock is like reviewing a restaurant. You don't expect it to be 100% perfect, but before it gets three or four stars you want it to be superior.

Nº **6**

BUY VALUE, NOT MARKET TRENDS
OR THE ECONOMIC OUTLOOK

A wise investor knows that the stock market is really a market of stocks. While a strong bull market may pull individual stocks along momentarily, ultimately it is the individual stocks that determine the market, not vice versa. All too many investors focus on the market trend or economic outlook. But individual stocks can rise in a bear market and fall in a bull market.

The stock market and the economy do not always march in lock step. Bear markets do not always coincide with recessions, and an overall decline in corporate earnings does not always cause a simultaneous decline in stock prices. So buy individual stocks, not the market trend or economic outlook.

N° 7

DIVERSIFY. IN STOCKS AND BONDS, AS IN MUCH ELSE, THERE IS SAFETY IN NUMBERS

No matter how careful you are, you can neither predict nor control the future. A hurricane or earthquake, a strike at a supplier, an unexpected technological advance by a competitor, or a government-ordered product recall, any one of these can cost a company millions of dollars. Then, too, what looked like such a well-managed company may turn out to have serious internal problems that weren't apparent when you bought the stock.

So you diversify?y industry, by risk, and by country. For example, if you search worldwide, you will find more bargains and possibly better bargains than in any single nation.

N° 8

DO YOUR HOMEWORK OR HIRE WISE EXPERTS TO HELP YOU

People will tell you: Investigate before you invest. Listen to them. Study companies to learn what makes them successful.

Remember, in most instances, you are buying either earnings or assets. In free-enterprise nations, earnings and assets together are major influences on the price of most stocks. The earnings on stock market indexes the fabled Dow Jones Industrials, for example, fluctuate around the replacement book value of the shares of the index. (That's the money it would take to replace the assets of the companies making up the index at today's costs.)

If you expect a company to grow and prosper, you are buying future earnings. You expect that earnings will go up, and because most stocks are valued on future earnings, you can expect the stock price may rise also.

If you expect a company to be acquired or

dissolved at a premium over its market price, you may be buying assets. Years ago Forbes regularly published lists of these so-called "loaded laggards!' But remember, there are far fewer of these companies today. Raiders have swept through the marketplace over the past 10 to 15 years: Be very suspicious of what they left behind.

N° 9

AGGRESSIVELY MONITOR YOUR INVESTMENTS

Expect and react to change. No bull market is permanent. No bear market is permanent. And there are no stocks that you can buy and forget. The pace of change is too great. Being relaxed, as Hooper advised, doesn't mean being complacent.

Consider, for example, just the 30 issues that comprise the Dow Jones Industrials. From 1978 through 1990, one of every three issues changed because the company was in decline, or was acquired, or went private, or went bankrupt. Look at the 100 largest industrials on Fortune magazine's list. In just seven years, 1983 through 1990, 30 dropped off the list. They merged with another giant company, or became too small for the top 100, or were acquired by a foreign company, or went private, or went out of business. Remember, no investment is forever.

N° 10

DON'T PANIC

Sometimes you won't have sold when everyone else is buying, and you'll be caught in a market crash such as we had in 1987. There you are, facing a 15% loss in a single day. Maybe more.

Don't rush to sell the next day. The time to sell is before the crash, not after. Instead, study your portfolio. If you didn't own these stocks now, would you buy them after the market crash? Chances are you would. So the only reason to sell them now is to buy other, more attractive stocks. If you can't find more attractive stocks, hold on to what you have.

N° 11

LEARN FROM YOUR MISTAKES

The only way to avoid mistakes is not to invest, which is the biggest mistake of all. So forgive yourself for your errors. Don't become discouraged, and certainly don't try to recoup your losses by taking bigger risks. Instead, turn each mistake into a learning experience. Determine exactly what went wrong and how you can avoid the same mistake in the future.

The investor who says, "This time is different," when in fact it's virtually a repeat of an earlier situation, has uttered among the four most costly words in the annals of investing.

The big difference between those who are successful and those who are not is that successful people learn from their mistakes and the mistakes of others.

N° 12

BEGIN WITH A PRAYER

If you begin with a prayer, you can think more clearly and make fewer mistakes.

N° 13

OUTPERFORMING THE MARKET
IS A DIFFICULT TASK

The challenge is not simply making better investment decisions than the average investor. The real challenge is making investment decisions that are better than those of the professionals who manage the big institutions.

Remember, the unmanaged market indexes such as the S&P 500 don't pay commissions to buy and sell stock. They don't pay salaries to securities analysts or portfolio managers. And, unlike the unmanaged indexes, investment companies are never 100% invested, because they need to have cash on hand to redeem shares.

So any investment company that consistently outperforms the market is actually doing a much better job than you might think. And if it not only consistently outperforms the market, but also does so by a significant degree, it is doing a superb job.

"...Success is a process of continually seeking answers to new questions."

N° 14

AN INVESTOR WHO HAS ALL THE ANSWERS DOESN'T EVEN UNDERSTAND ALL THE QUESTIONS

A cocksure approach to investing will lead, probably sooner than later, to disappointment if not outright disaster. Even if we can identify an unchanging handful of investing principles, we cannot apply these rules to an unchanging universe of investments or an unchanging economic and political environment. Everything is in a constant state of change, and the wise investor recognizes that success is a process of continually seeking answers to new questions.

N° 15
THERE'S NO FREE LUNCH

This principle covers an endless list of admonitions. Never invest on sentiment. The company that gave you your first job, or built the first car you ever owned, or sponsored a favorite television show of long ago may be a fine company. But that doesn't mean its stock is a fine investment. Even if the corporation is truly excellent, prices of its shares may be too high.

Never invest in an initial public offering (IPO) to "save" the commission. That commission is built into the price of the stock, the reason why most new stocks decline in value after the offering. This does not mean you should never buy an IPO.

Never invest solely on a tip. Why, that's obvious, you might say. It is. But you would be surprised how many investors, people who are well educated and successful, do exactly this. Unfortunately, there is something psychologically compelling about a tip. Its very nature suggests inside information, a way to turn a fast profit.

N° 16

DO NOT BE FEARFUL OR NEGATIVE TOO OFTEN

And now the last principle. Do not be fearful or negative too often. For 100 years, optimists have carried the day in U.S. stocks. Even in the dark '70s, many professional money managers and many individual investors too made money in stocks, especially those of smaller companies.

There will, of course, be corrections, perhaps even crashes. But, over time, our studies indicate stocks do go up...and up... and up. With the fall of communism and the sharply reduced threat of nuclear war, it appears that the U.S. and some form of an economically united Europe may be about to enter the most glorious period in their history.

As national economies become more integrated and interdependent, as communication becomes easier and cheaper, business is likely to boom. Trade and travel will grow. Wealth will increase. And stock prices should rise accordingly.

By the time the 21st century begins it's just around the corner, you know? think there is at least an even chance that the Dow Jones Industrials may have reached 6,000, perhaps more.

Chances are that certain other indexes will have grown even more. Despite all the current gloom about the economy, and about the future, more people will have more money than ever before in history. And much of it will be invested in stocks.

And throughout this wonderful time, the basic rules of building wealth by investing in stocks will hold true. In this century or the next it's still "Buy low, sell high."

Recommendes Readings

• Warren Buffett Talks to MBA Students by Warren Buffett

• Stock Options: The Greatest Wealth Building Tool Ever Invented by Daniel Mollat

• You Can Still Make It In The Market by Nicolas Darvas

• Show Me Your Options (The Guide to Complete Confidence for Every Stock and Options Trader Seeking Consistent, Predictable , Returns by Steve Burns, Christopher Ebert

• Invest like a Billionaire: If you are not watching the best investor in the world, who are you watching?

• Back to School: Question & Answer Session with Business Students by Warren Buffett

• New Trader, Rich Trader: How to Make Money in the Stock Market by Ste!e Burns

Available at
www.bnpublishing.com

Made in the USA
Las Vegas, NV
14 August 2022

53215421R00038